REVISION ACTIVITIES HOW TO REVISE FOR ALL SUBJECTS

Active Revision Techniques to Unlock Exam Success

By

School Success Publishing

A Brief Introduction

1. Once you've organised what you want to revise, it can be tricky to know how to revise. These useful templates will fix this and have you learning the content and techniques you need in no time.

2. This resource contains 10 templates that can be applied to revising any topic.

3. For each template there is an example of how to use it to revise effectively.

4. Give each activity a go for your different subjects to see which ones suit your learning style and topics best. Some are good for very early revision, like Brain dumps or Cornell notes. Others, like essay planning, are better for later on when you know more content and want to practice exam style answers.

5. And that's it. No more instructions are needed. Get revising and good luck.

6. Remember, before you start revising you need to plan carefully to cover the content of your courses. If you need help with this, why not try the GCSE Revision Planner by School Success Publishing, also available on Amazon. This resource will have you organised with revision schedules in no time.

This resource was produced by a teacher with over 20 years of experience helping students just like you to prepare for and ace their GCSE and A-Level exams.

Glossary

Retrieval practice is a study technique that involves recalling information from memory without looking at your notes or other sources. It helps you to improve your long-term retention and understanding of the material, as well as to identify any gaps in your knowledge.

Dual coding is a study technique that involves using both words and images to help you remember information. For example, you can use diagrams, charts, graphs, symbols, or colours to represent key concepts or facts. Dual coding can improve your memory and understanding by creating multiple associations in your brain.

Spacing is a study technique that involves spreading out your revision sessions over time, rather than cramming them all at once. Spacing helps you remember information better and avoid forgetting.

Cornell Notes

Cornell note-taking is a popular note-taking method for taking, organising, and summarising notes. This method typically results in better overall comprehension. Take pages from you exercise books on a particular topic and turn them into a page or Cornell notes.

CORNELL NOTES

Topic: Animal Farm Methods	Name: _____
Source: ——— Bitesize ———	Class: ——— English ———
	Date: _____

Questions/Main Ideas	Notes
Irony	**Verbal Irony** E.g. 'All animals are equal, but some animals are more equal than others' **Dramatic Irony** 'Besides, in those days they had been slaves and now they were free' **Situational Irony** from man to pig, and from pig to man again; but already it was impossible to say which was which
Allegory	**Political allegory** The symbols used are obvious – as you would expect in an allegory. The farm represents Russia; Napoleon as Stalin. The satire also makes complex political events, like the German invasion of Russia (Battle of the Windmill) easy for us to understand.

Summary

Orwell's irony creates satire of the manipulative and controlling pigs' regime relating to the allegory of government's exploitation of their people.

CORNELL NOTES

Topic: _____

Source: _____

Name: _____

Class: History

Date: _____

Questions/Main Ideas

Notes

Summary

CORNELL NOTES

Topic: _____

Source: _____

Name: _____

Class: _____

Date: _____

Questions/Main Ideas	Notes

Summary

CORNELL NOTES

Topic: _____

Source: _____

Name: _____

Class: _____

Date: _____

Questions/Main Ideas	Notes

Summary

CORNELL NOTES

Topic: _____

Source: _____

Name: _____

Class: _____

Date: _____

Questions/Main Ideas	Notes

Summary

CORNELL NOTES

Topic: _____

Source: _____

Name: _____

Class: _____

Date: _____

Questions/Main Ideas	Notes

Summary

CORNELL NOTES

Topic: _____

Source: _____

Name: _____

Class: _____

Date: _____

Questions/Main Ideas	Notes

Summary

CORNELL NOTES

Topic: _____

Source: _____

Name: _____

Class: _____

Date: _____

Questions/Main Ideas	Notes

Summary

CORNELL NOTES

Topic: _____

Source: _____

Name: _____

Class: _____

Date: _____

Questions/Main Ideas	Notes

Summary

CORNELL NOTES

Topic: _____

Source: _____

Name: _____

Class: _____

Date: _____

Questions/Main Ideas	Notes

Summary

CORNELL NOTES

Topic: _____

Source: _____

Name: _____

Class: _____

Date: _____

Questions/Main Ideas	Notes

Summary

Brain Dump

Often, the best place to start with a topic is by writing down everything you think you know about a topic with no restrictions. This is called a brain dump. Don't worry about having any structure or connections. If you want, you can add these afterwards and use some colour coding to connect the topics. After you've written everything you know on the topic, consult your notes to see what you've missed. These can
then become priorities for revision.

Biology- Cells

cell wall

Plant vs animal cells

membrane
mitosis

Specialised
cells

cytoplasm

meiosis

chloroplasts

osmosis

nucleus

Organised Recall

Try retrieving your knowledge in a more organised way. First break your topic down into three main subtopics. Recall as much knowledge as you can from memory in categories and then use notes to add what you've forgotten. Repeat this for the same topic at different stages of your revision to see what you have retained by comparing it to your first one where it is complete as you topped it up with notes. This is called spacing and by revisiting multiple times an intervals, you should retain more each time. You can hand draw more boxes where necessary and of course use colour coding.

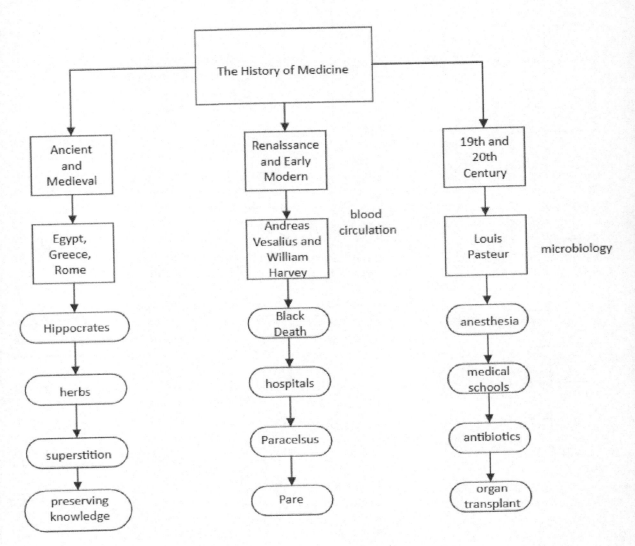

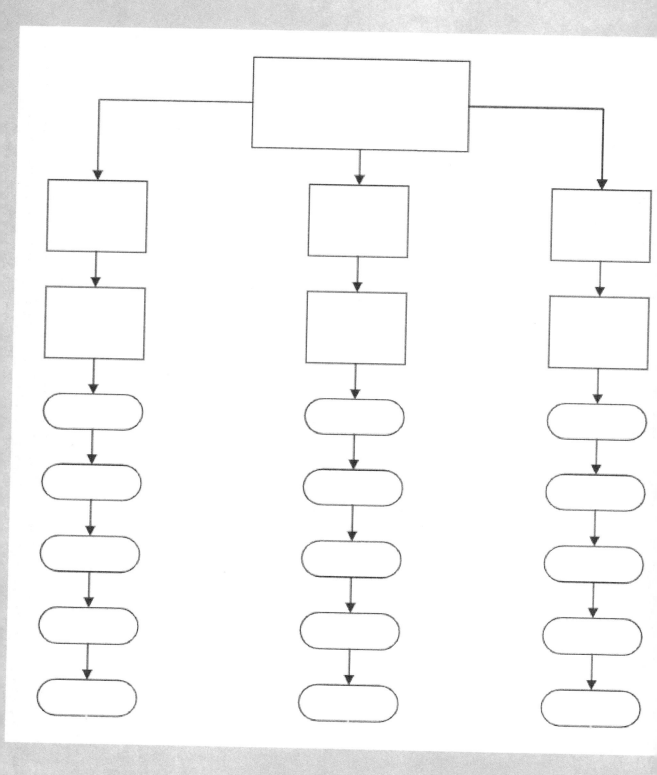

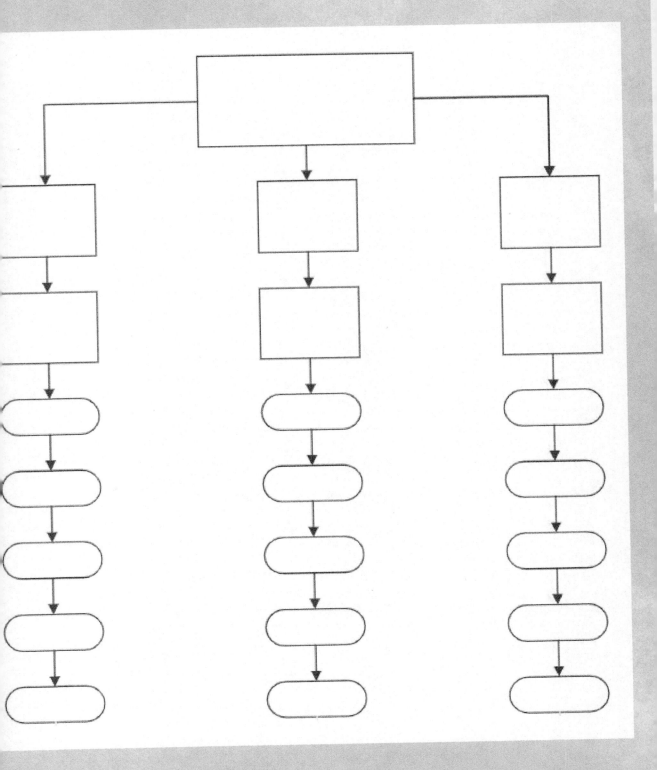

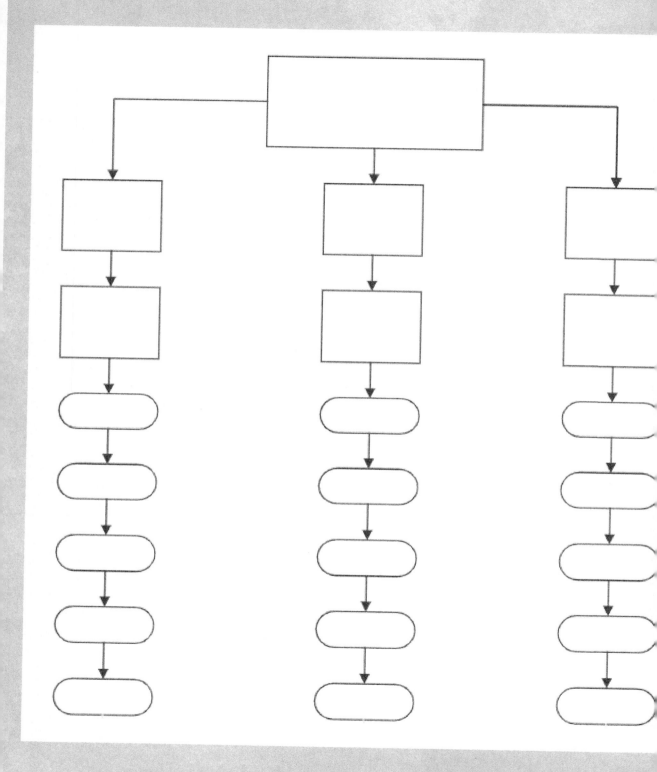

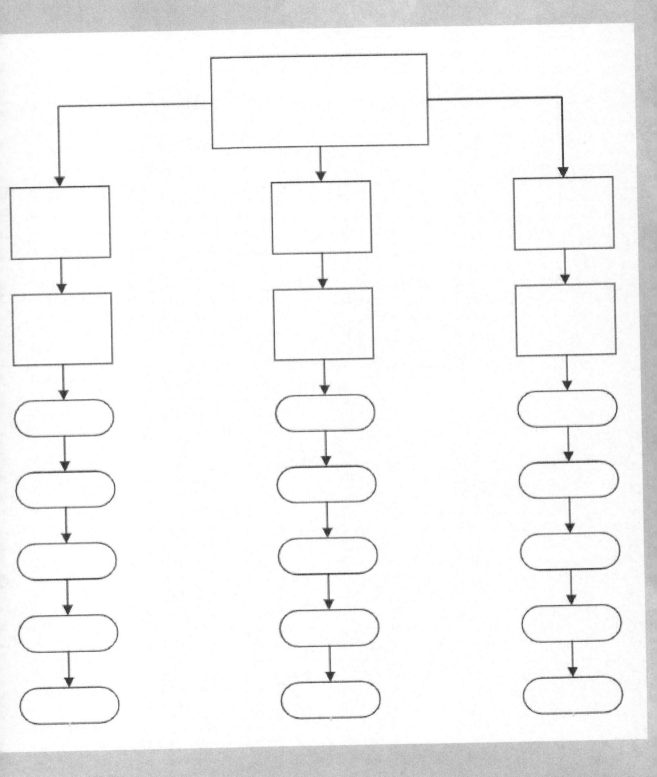

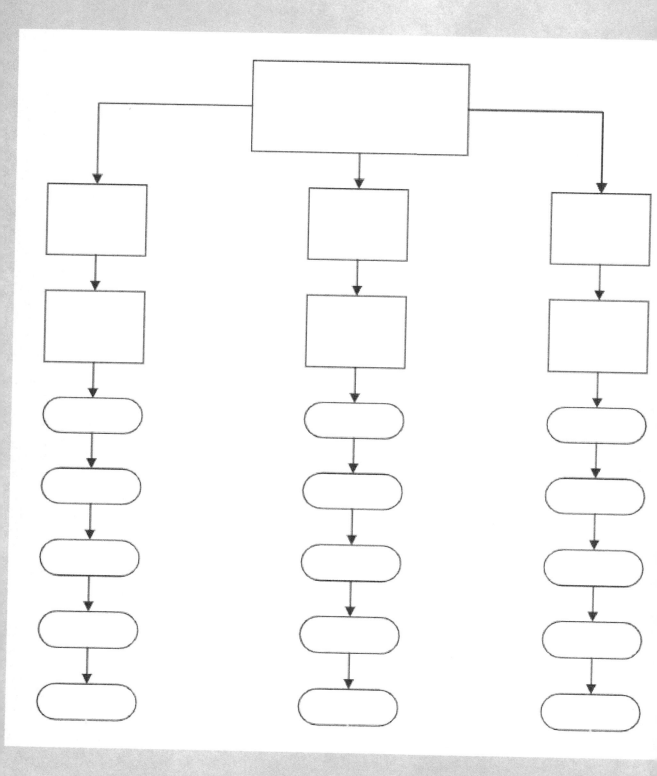

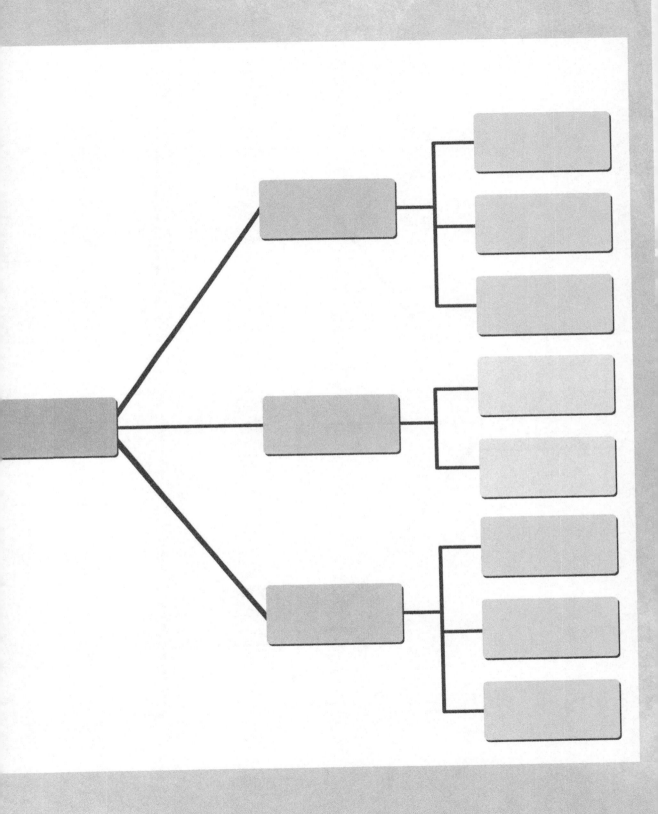

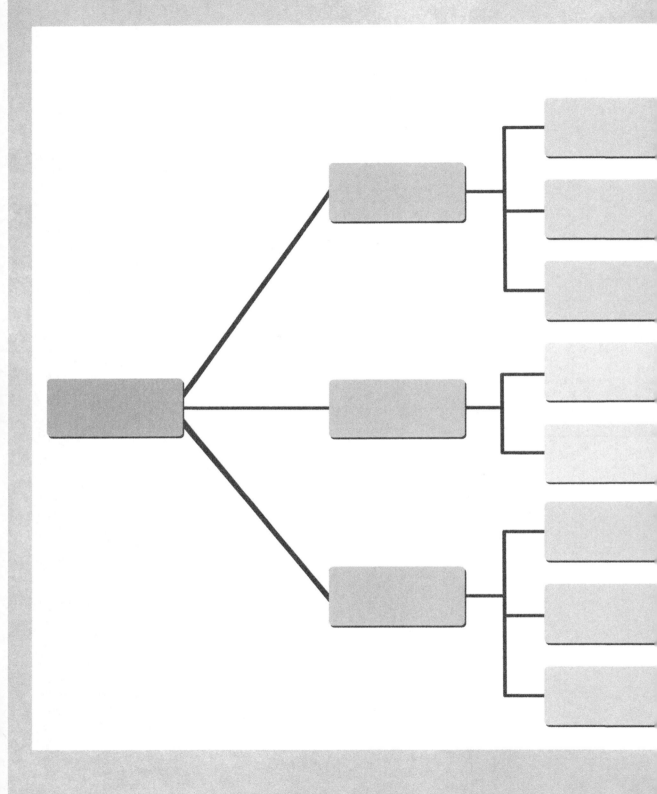

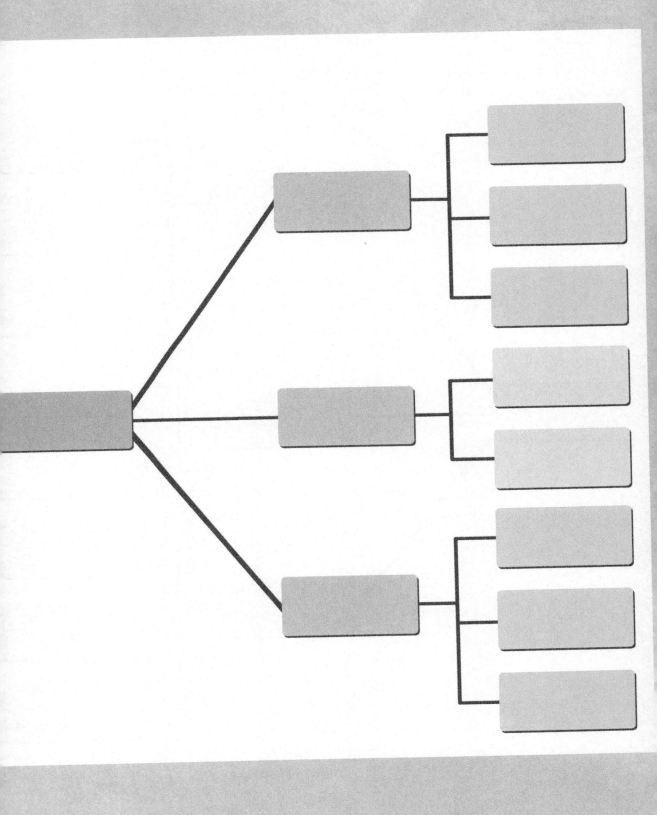

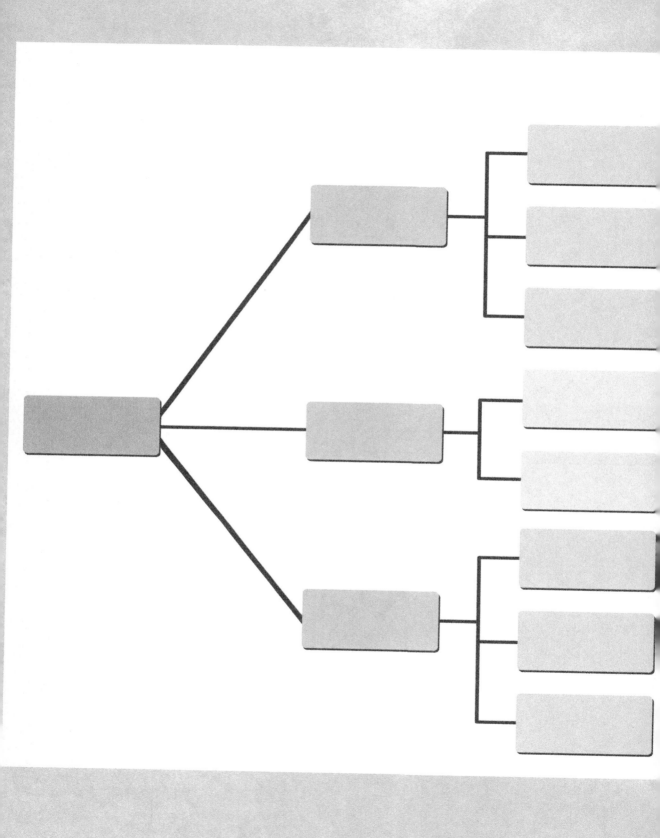

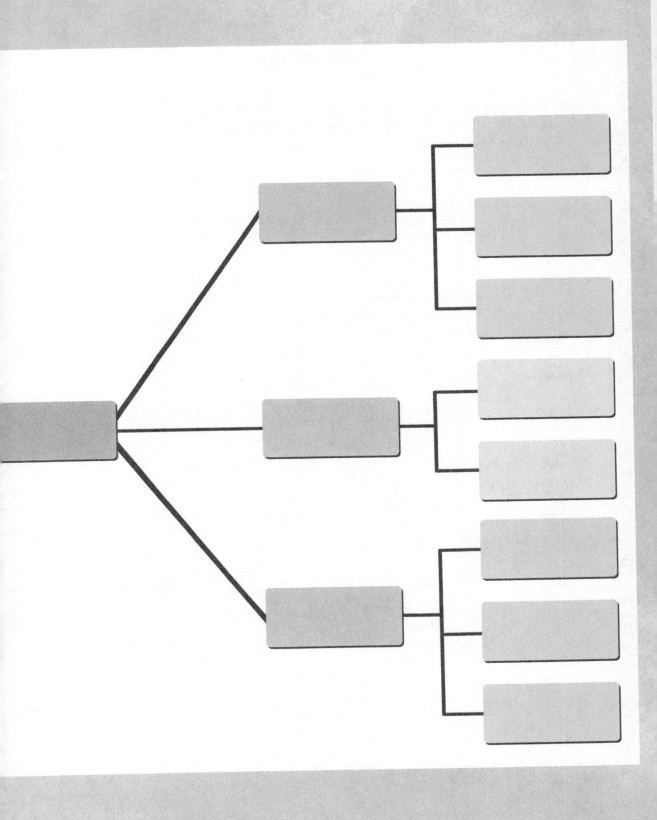

Mindmaps

This might be one you've tried before, but mindmaps are great ways to recall and organise topics. Codify information with colour, images and symbols to aid recall.

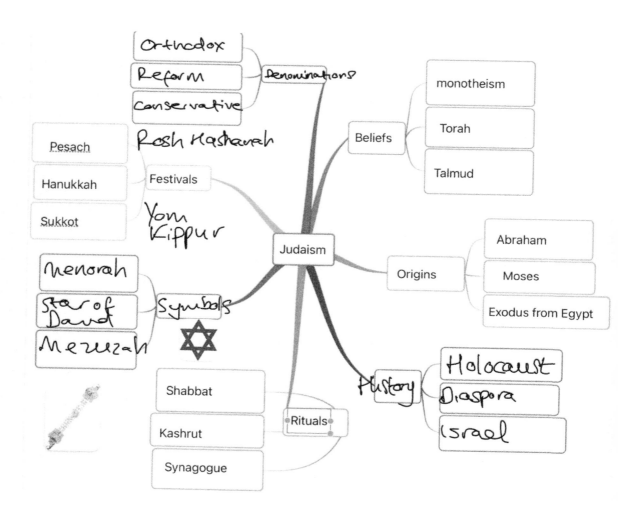

Orthodox
Reform
Conservative — Denominations

monotheism
Torah — Beliefs
Talmud

Rosh Hashanah

Pesach
Hanukkah — Festivals
Sukkot

Yom Kippur

Judaism

Abraham
Origins — Moses
Exodus from Egypt

menorah
Star of David — Symbols
Mezuzah

Shabbat
Kashrut — Rituals
Synagogue

History — Holocaust
Diaspora
Israel

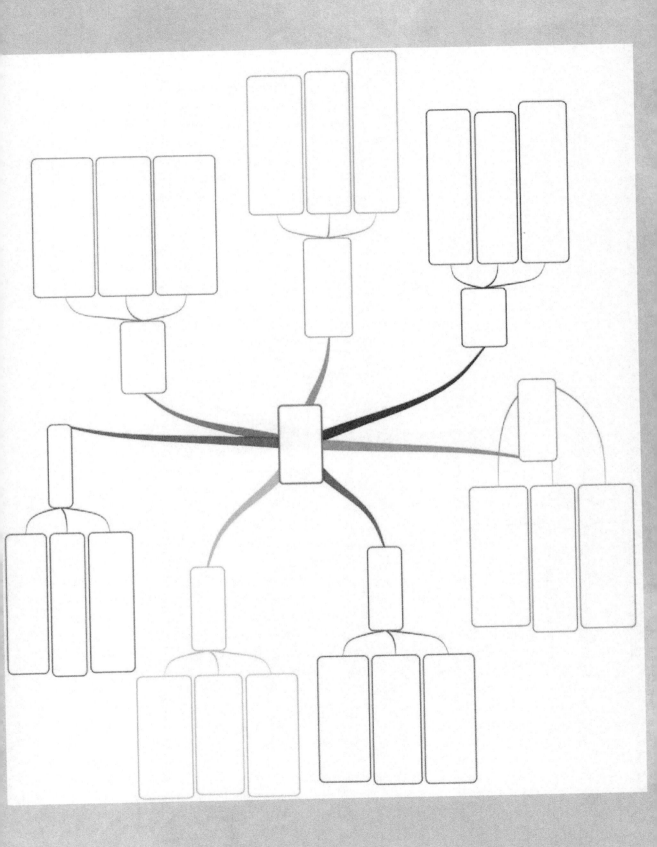

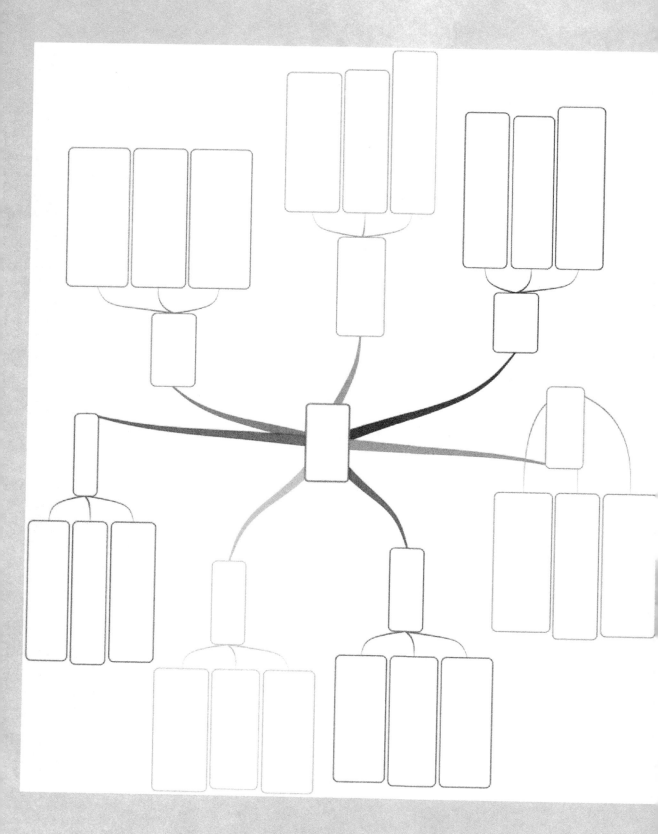

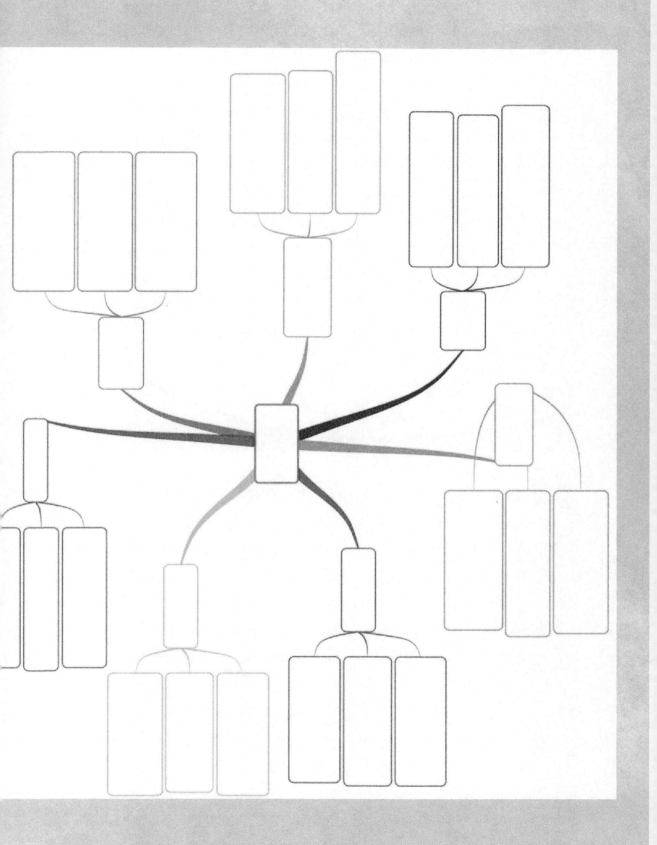

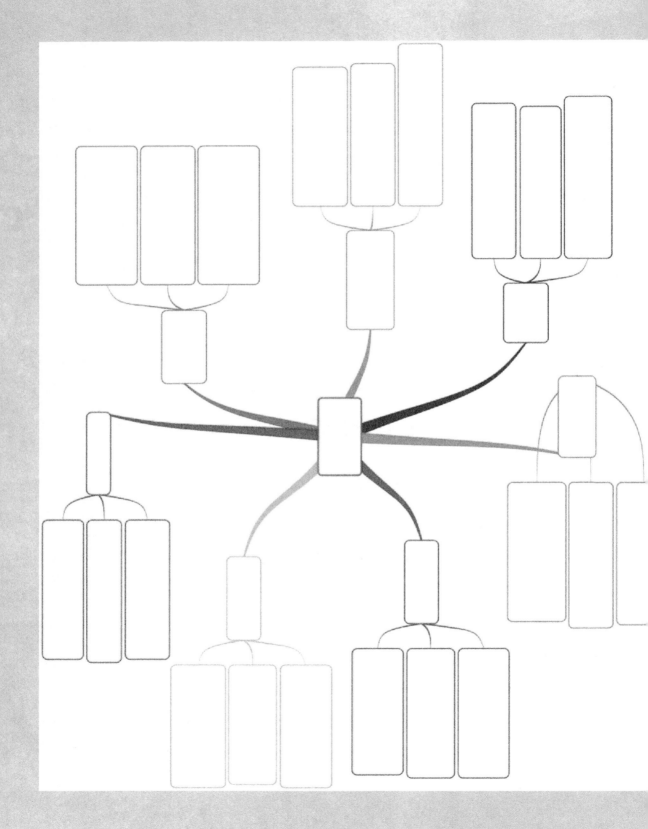

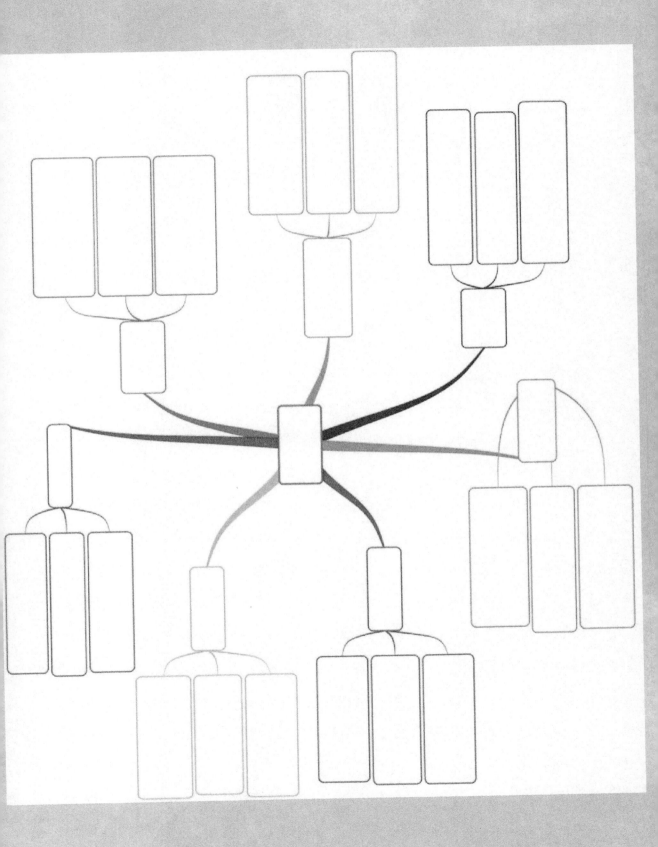

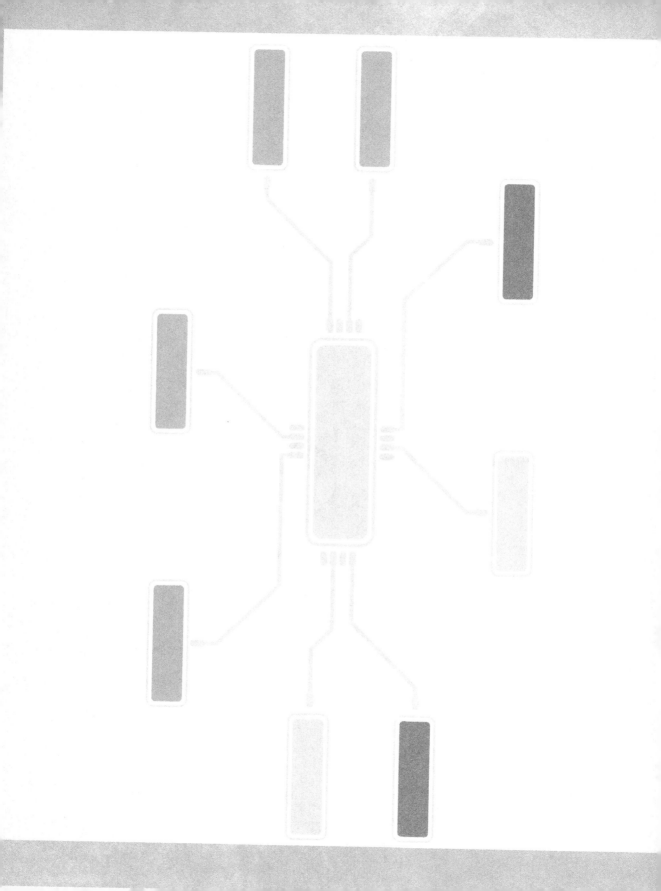

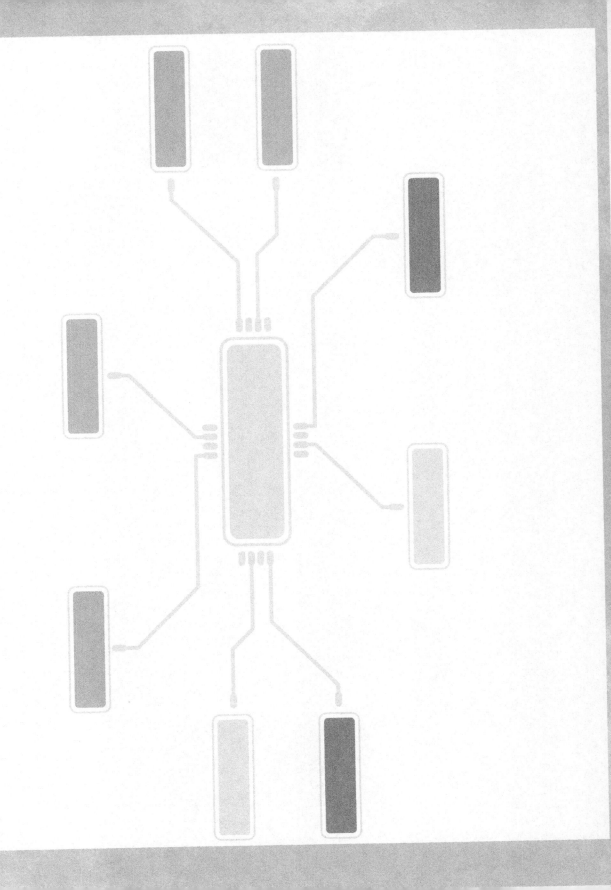

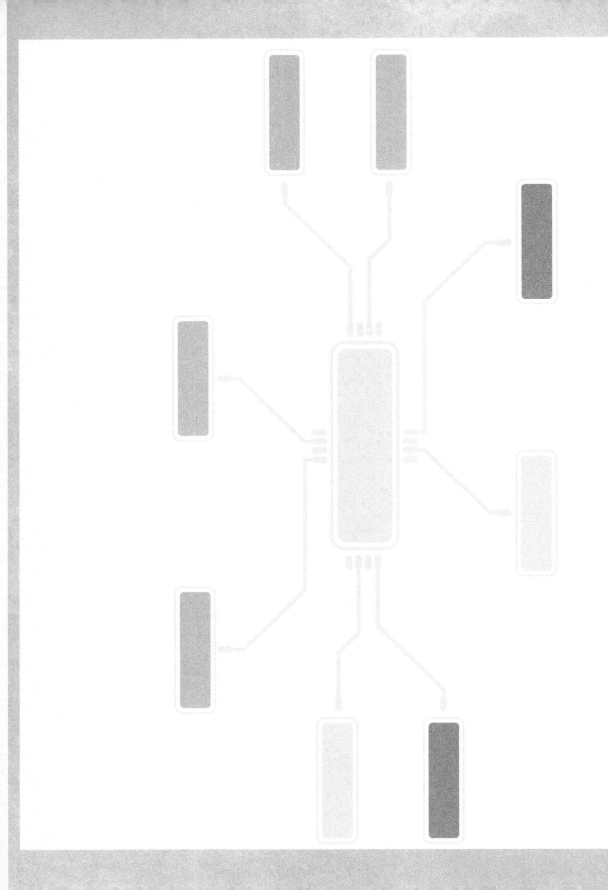

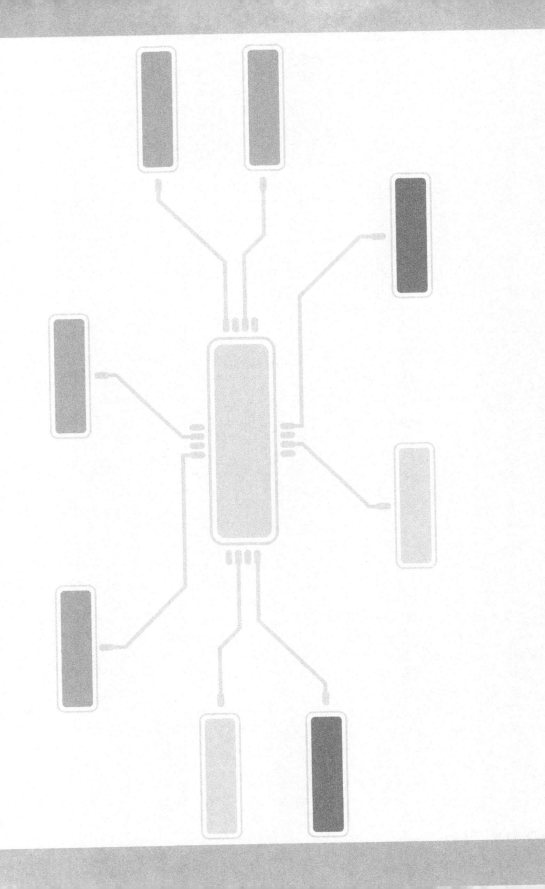

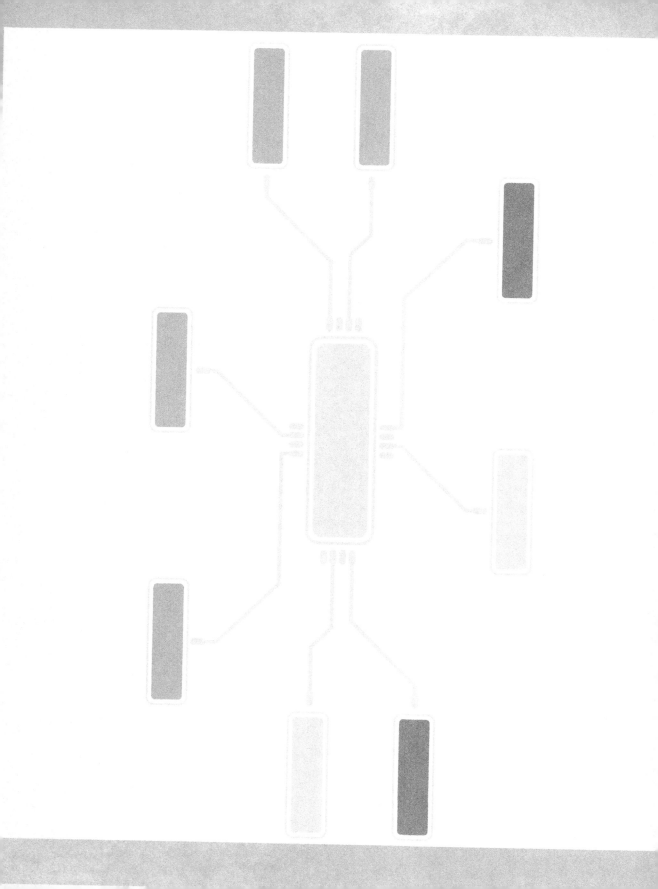

Knowledge Organiser

When you want to go a bit deeper with the knowledge, try a knowledge organiser. For a topic you need to know a lot of detail on, break the topic into 4 key areas and give each a title. For each, note down specifics and examples. This could be worked sums, quotations, key words, definitions etc. Include images and colour where you can. Try doing this from memory. Or if you're not ready use it to condense notes down to the essentials that need to be learnt so you can practice recalling the knowledge. You can further divide the boxes to suit your needs.

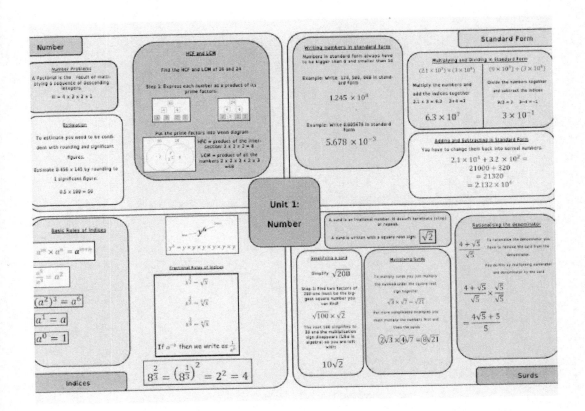

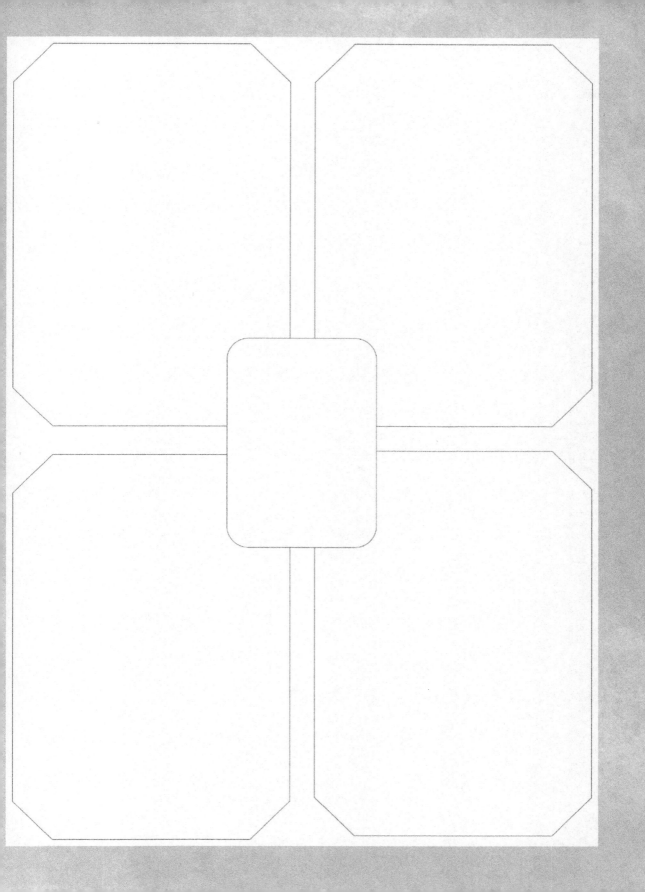

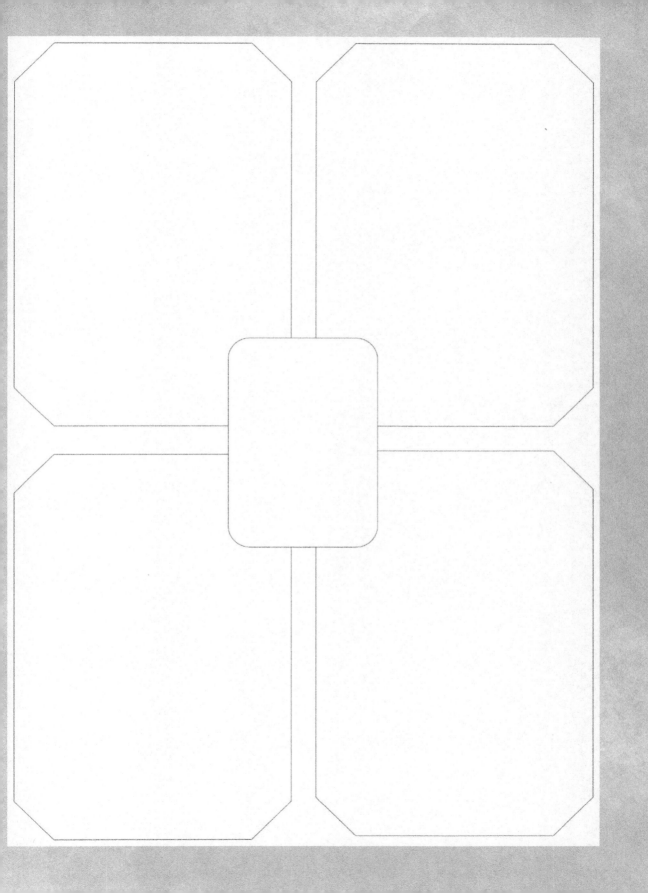

Revision Clock

Another way of organizing knowledge is to lay it out as a clock. This can help to give structure and suggest sequencing where this is important. This can make this helpful for revising processes or linked concepts.

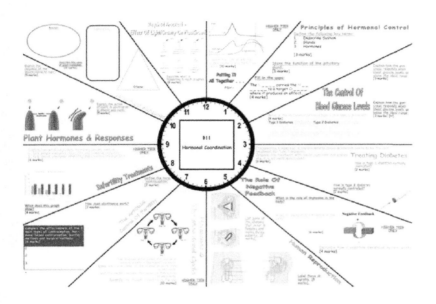

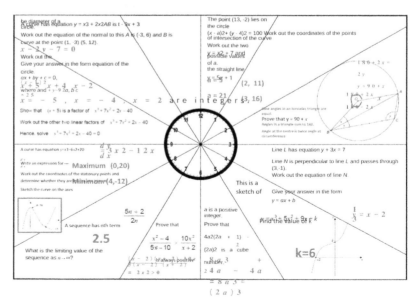

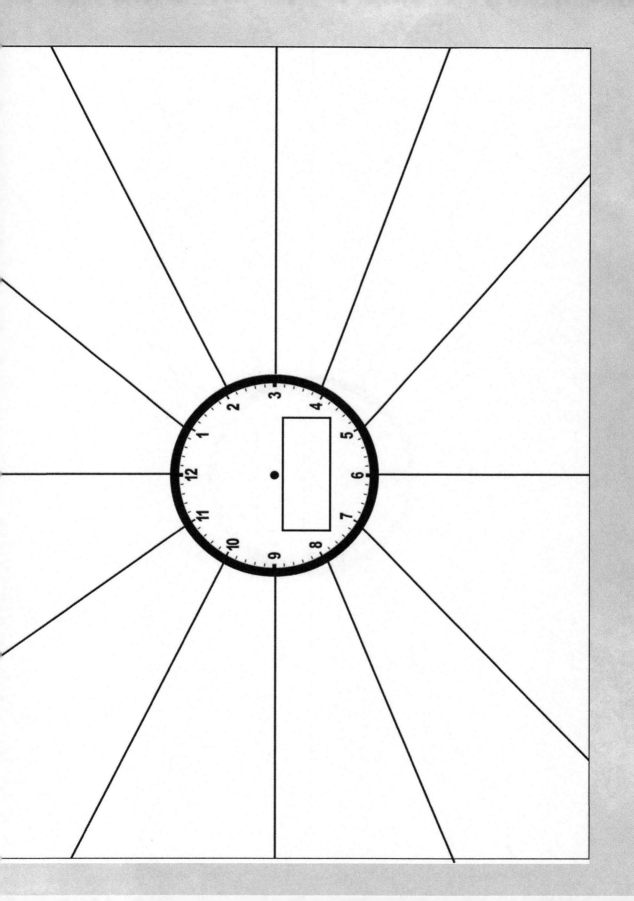

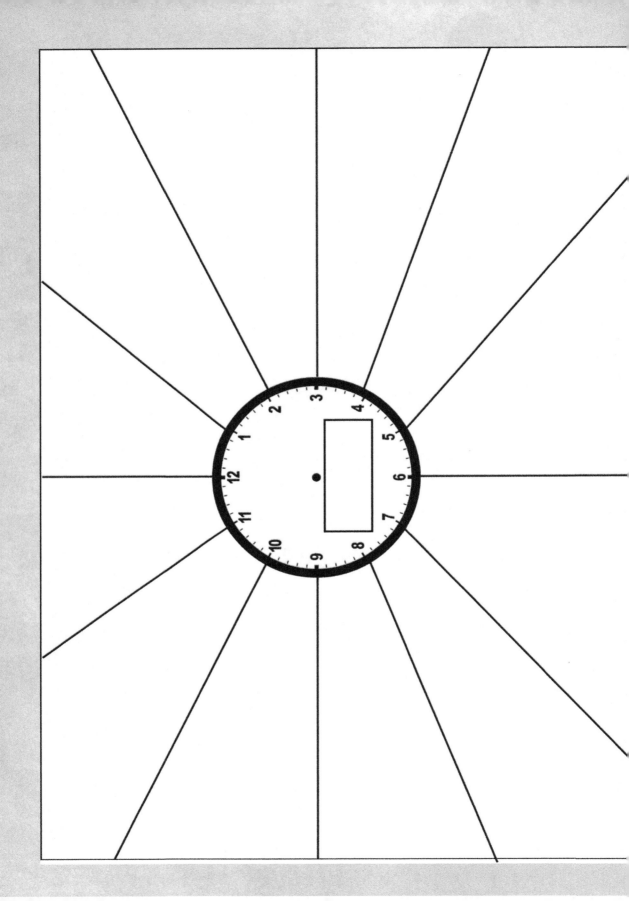

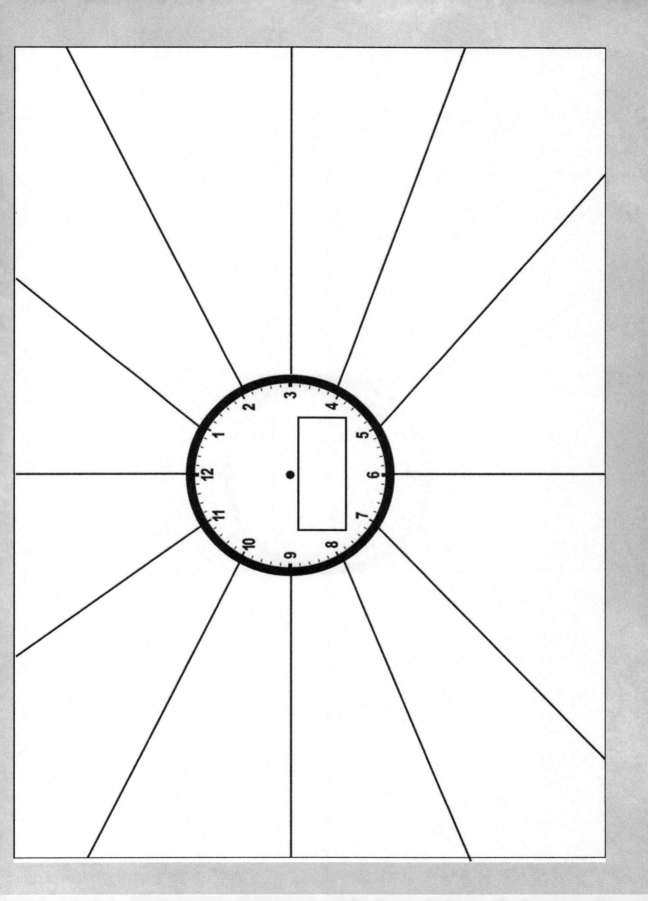

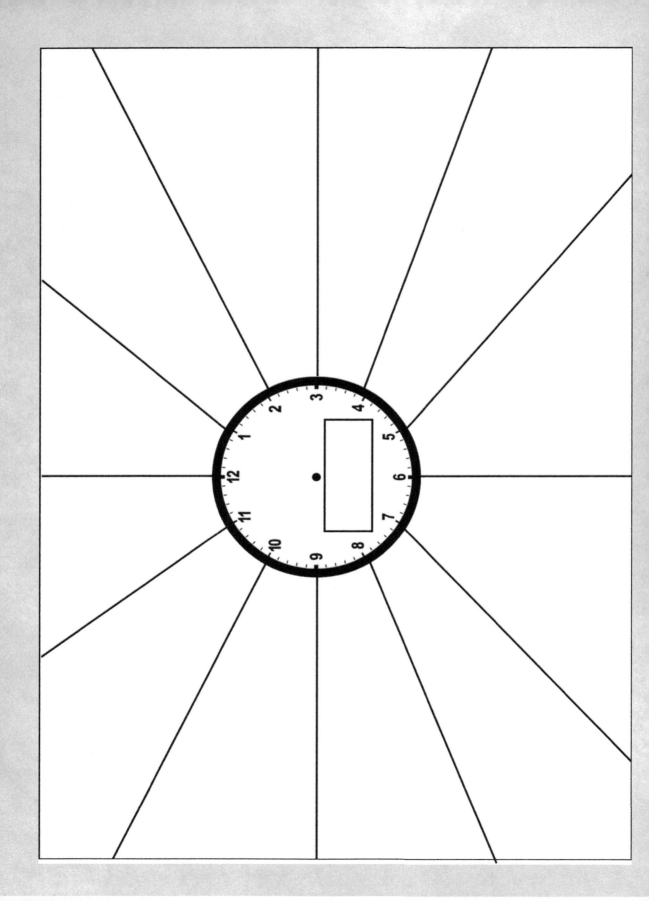

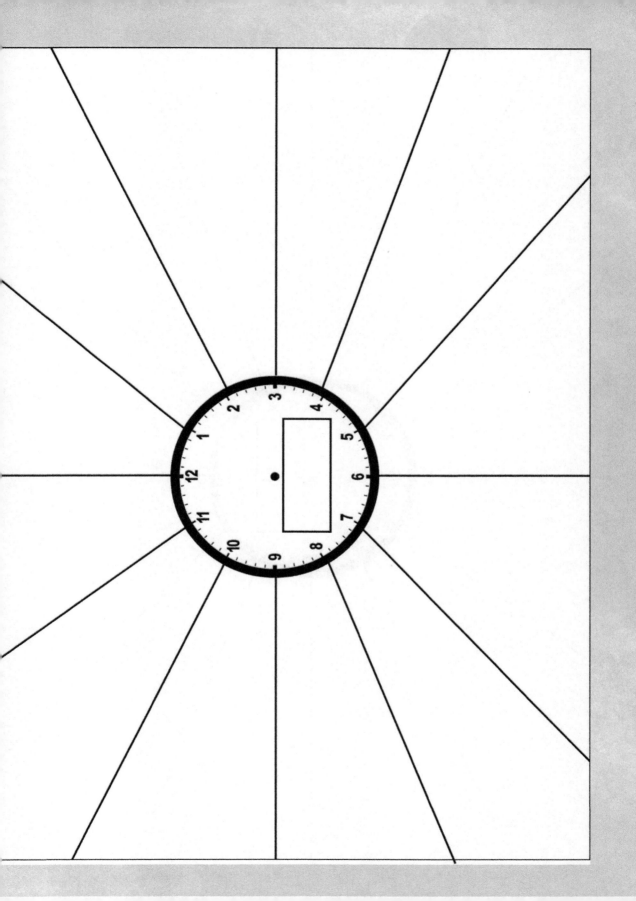

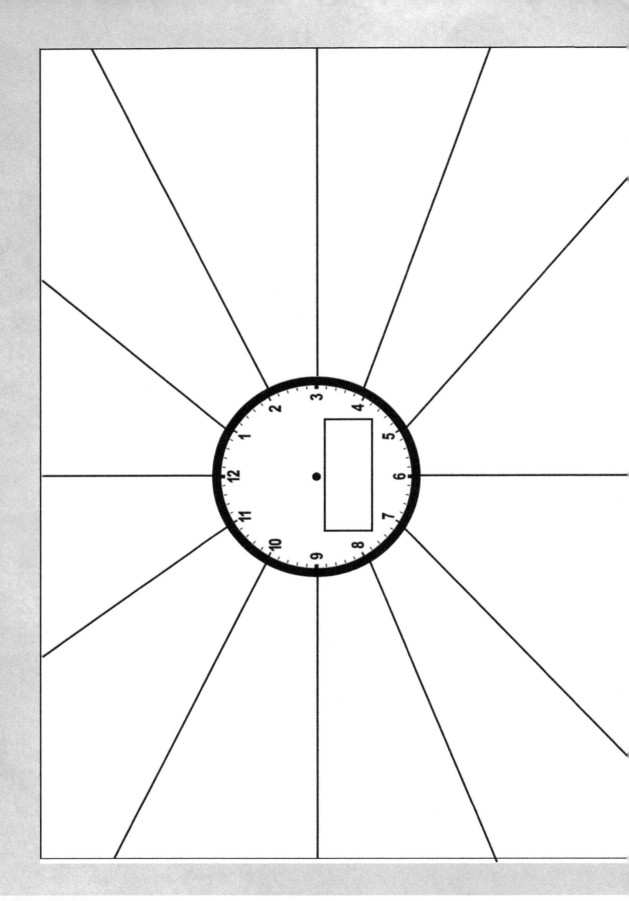

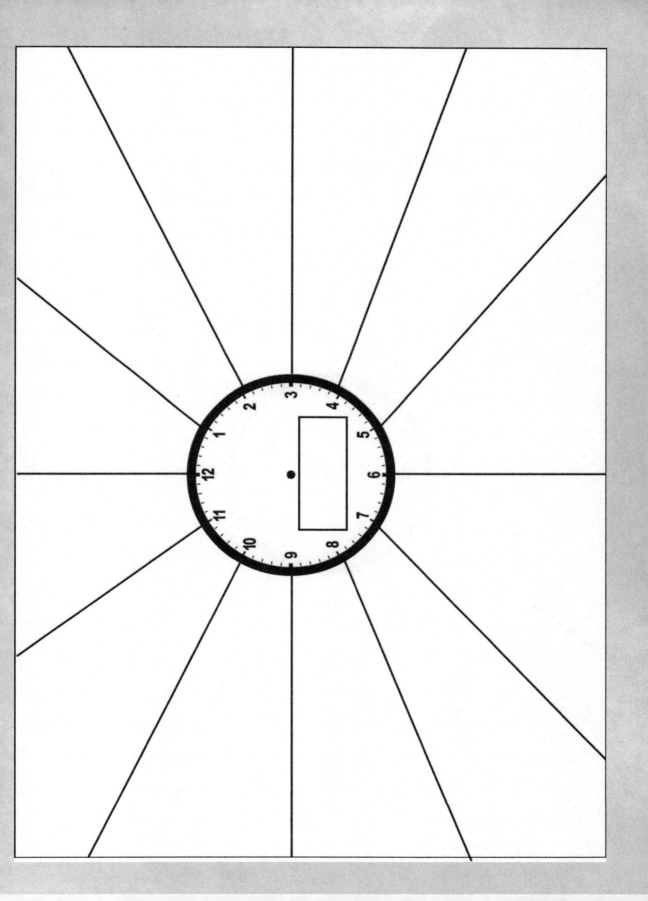

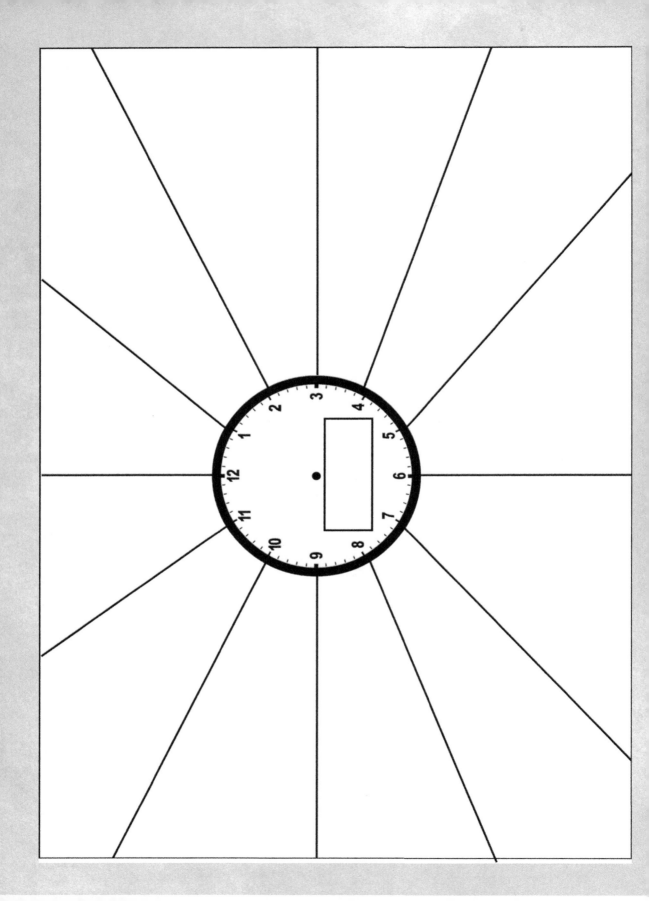

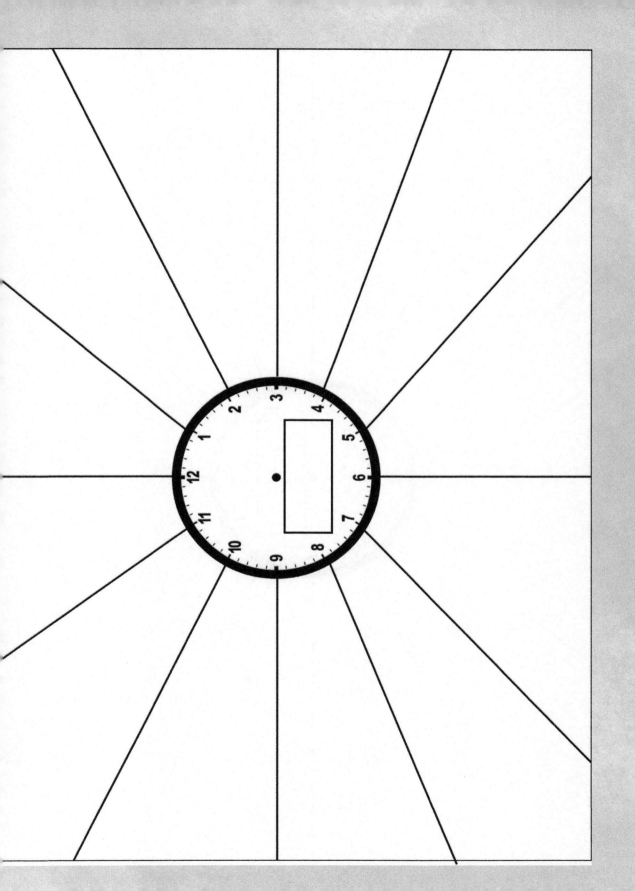

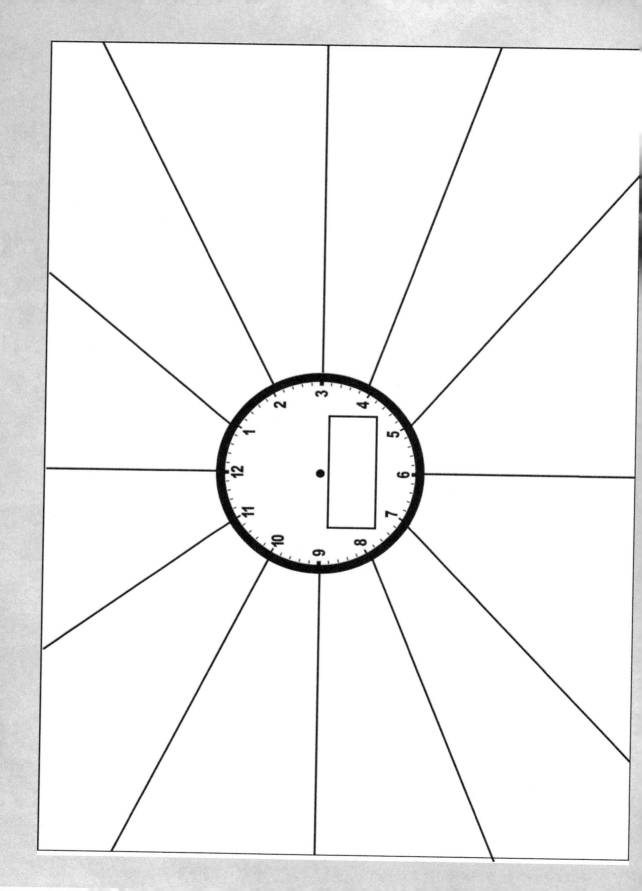

Priority Pyramid

What about when you want to get a lot of information down to the manageable essentials to learn? Perhaps one for a little further into the revision process, you can use these inverted pyramids to condense down the knowledge you need into its essentials. Do this by recalling from memory or using notes to complete the top tier and reducing down in stages. The must know goes at the top and then nice to know at the bottom. These could be useful for stories and events to learn, such as those in History or English Literature. Or properties of elements or materials such as below.

Properties and uses of MDF

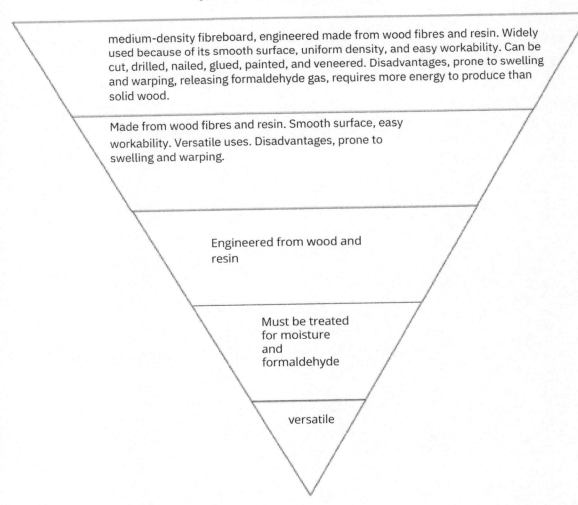

medium-density fibreboard, engineered made from wood fibres and resin. Widely used because of its smooth surface, uniform density, and easy workability. Can be cut, drilled, nailed, glued, painted, and veneered. Disadvantages, prone to swelling and warping, releasing formaldehyde gas, requires more energy to produce than solid wood.

Made from wood fibres and resin. Smooth surface, easy workability. Versatile uses. Disadvantages, prone to swelling and warping.

Engineered from wood and resin

Must be treated for moisture and formaldehyde

versatile

Honeycomb Revision

This method is great for when you want to test yourself with retrieval practice and make connections across topics. Start somewhere in the middle with the key concept. Fill the honeycomb outwards with each touching hexagon connecting in some way to those it touches. Use some coding, like colour, to aid memory.

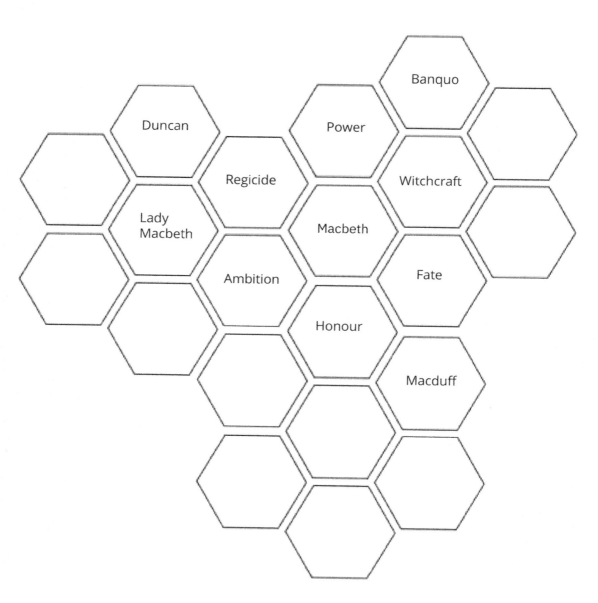

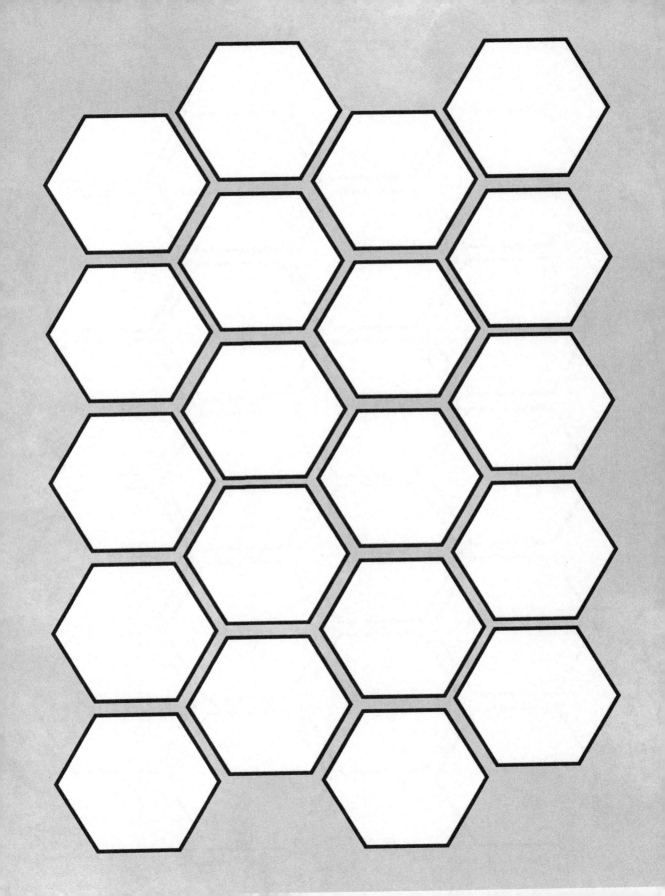

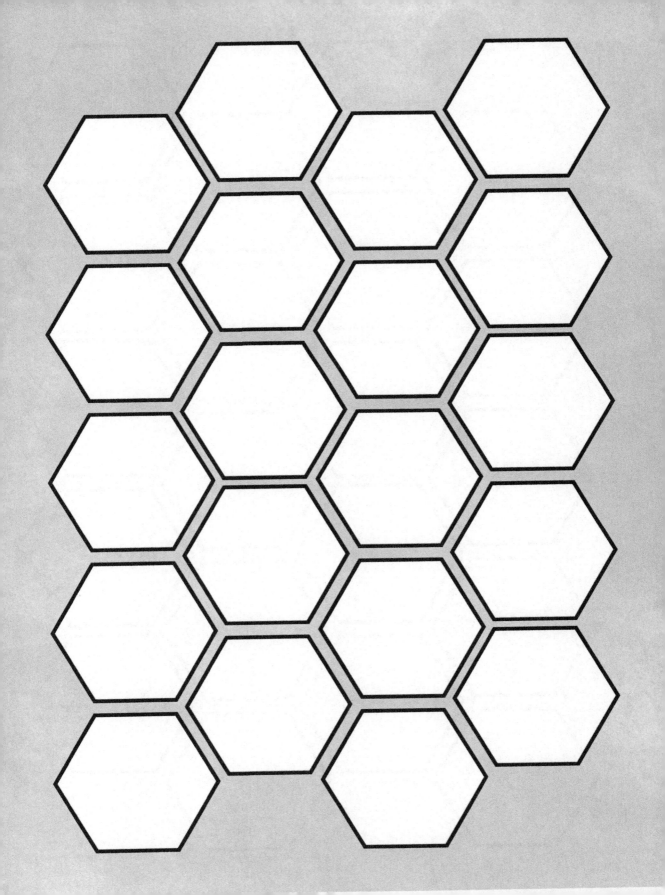

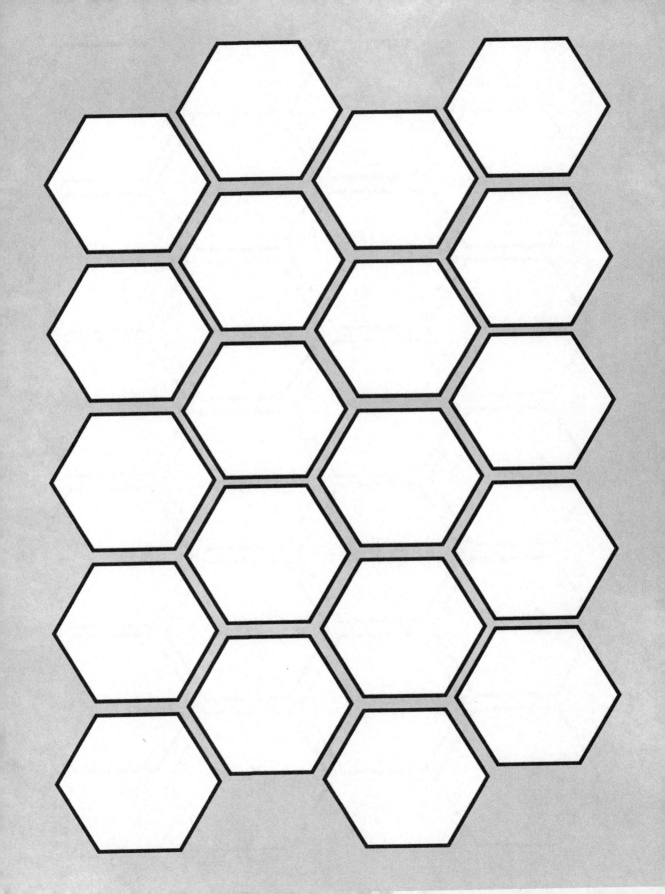

Long Answer/Essay Planning

An important part of revision is practicing how to apply the knowledge you've been committing to memory. For some subjects this will require longer answers with an argument. Use the essay template to practise planning arguments for questions that require sustained answers.

ESSAY PLANNER

SUBJECT   PE

Essay Prompt/Title

Explain the principles of training and how they can be applied in a training program for a competitive athlete. Provide specific examples to support your explanation.

Introduction

Thesis Statement

The principles of training are fundamental concepts in designing effective training programs for athletes. These principles guide coaches and athletes in achieving specific fitness goals while minimizing the risk of injury.

Body

Paragraph 1

If a competitive sprinter aims to improve their explosiveness off the starting blocks, their training program should focus on sprint-specific drills, like explosive starts and acceleration techniques.

Paragraph 2

Progressive For example, a weightlifter looking to increase their strength might progressively increase the weight they lift during resistance training sessions.

Paragraph 3

Variety/ Introducing variety into a training program can prevent variation boredom, reduce the risk of overuse injuries, and enhance overall fitness. A long-distance runner might incorporate cross-training activities like cycling or yoga to add variety to their routine

Conclusion

In summary, a sprinter might use specificity by focusing on sprint-related drills, progressively overload by increasing sprint repetitions, incorporate variety with different sprint training methods, and prioritize rest and recovery to prevent burnout. By understanding and applying these principles, athletes and coaches can optimize training programs for improved performance.

ESSAY PLANNER

SUBJECT _____

Essay Prompt/Title

Body

Paragraph 1

Paragraph 2

Paragraph 3

Introduction

Hook

Background

Thesis Statement

Conclusion

ESSAY PLANNER

SUBJECT _____

Essay Prompt/Title

Body

Paragraph 1

Introduction

Hook

Paragraph 2

Background

Paragraph 3

Thesis Statement

Conclusion

ESSAY PLANNER

SUBJECT _____

Essay Prompt/Title

Body

Paragraph 1

Paragraph 2

Paragraph 3

Introduction

Hook

Background

Thesis Statement

Conclusion

ESSAY PLANNER

SUBJECT _____

Essay Prompt/Title

Body

Paragraph 1

Paragraph 2

Introduction

Hook

Background

Thesis Statement

Paragraph 3

Conclusion

ESSAY PLANNER

SUBJECT _____

Essay Prompt/Title

Body

Paragraph 1

Paragraph 2

Paragraph 3

Introduction

Hook

Background

Thesis Statement

Conclusion

ESSAY PLANNER

SUBJECT _____

Essay Prompt/Title

Introduction

Hook

Background

Thesis Statement

Body

Paragraph 1

Paragraph 2

Paragraph 3

Conclusion

ESSAY PLANNER

SUBJECT _____

Essay Prompt/Title

Introduction

Hook

Background

Thesis Statement

Body

Paragraph 1

Paragraph 2

Paragraph 3

Conclusion

ESSAY PLANNER

SUBJECT _____

Essay Prompt/Title

Body

Paragraph 1

Paragraph 2

Introduction

Hook

Background

Thesis Statement

Paragraph 3

Conclusion

ESSAY PLANNER

SUBJECT _____

Essay Prompt/Title

Body

Paragraph 1

Paragraph 2

Introduction

Hook

Background

Paragraph 3

Thesis Statement

Conclusion

ESSAY PLANNER

SUBJECT _____

Essay Prompt/Title

Body

Paragraph 1

Paragraph 2

Introduction

Hook

Paragraph 3

Background

Thesis Statement

Conclusion

Flash Cards

Flash cards are small cards that have a question on one side and an answer on the other.

They are a useful tool for revising for exams, as they help you test your knowledge and recall information quickly. To use flash cards effectively, you should follow these steps:

- Write down the key facts or concepts that you need to remember for each subject on separate cards. You can use different colours or symbols to categorise them by topic or difficulty.
- Shuffle the cards and pick one at random. Read the question and try to answer it without looking at the other side. If you are unsure, you can use a hint or a mnemonic to help you.
- Check the answer on the back of the card and see if you got it right. If you did, put the card in a pile of correct cards. If you didn't, put the card in a pile of incorrect cards.
- Repeat this process until you have gone through all the cards. Then, review the incorrect cards and try to learn from your mistakes. You can also mix the correct and incorrect cards and test yourself again.
- Keep practising with flash cards until you feel confident about your knowledge and can answer most of the questions correctly.

Front	Back
What is the chemical formula for sulphuric acid?	H_2SO_4

Printed in Great Britain
by Amazon